A
Journey
— to —
Ministry

Discover Your Calling, Purpose, and Destiny

Jamie Morgan

A Journey to Ministry
by Jamie Morgan

Printed in the United States of America

ISBN: 978-1718684096

DEDICATION

I dedicate this book to *You*, Lord Jesus. My prayer is that the story of my journey to ministry will inspire, encourage, and challenge my beautiful granddaughters, Claire Abigail and Hannah Jane, my treasured Life Church family, and men and women everywhere, to answer Your call on their lives.

—JM

TABLE OF CONTENTS

Part One
God Calls Me to Ministry

FOREWORD

In the classroom, she is a passionate student—especially in discussions that smack of compromise, lack of faith, lack of love, or lack of spiritual zeal. As a researcher, she is avid—not only with books in the library but also in conducting her own original research, up close and personal, on-site, and in face-to-face interviews.

As a Gospel witness, she knows no stranger—when the Lord opens the door, she will open her mouth. As a disciple-maker, she is a cheerleader—spurring others on in following Jesus! As a pastor, she is a mama bear—fighting to protect her cubs from danger. As a leader, she casts a bold vision and confidently inspires others—to "Go for it!" In the pulpit, she is a firebrand—proclaiming with power the promises of God. And in prayer, she is a warrior—having been called by God to help turn the Church back to fervent prayer.

This is Pastor Jamie Morgan, whom I have had the joy of witnessing in all of these roles!

It started for me several years ago, when I had her in my doctorate of ministry class, Biblical Theology of Women in Leadership. Her two papers for that class were so excellent, they became models, which I post online for other students to emulate.

The following year, I had the honor of serving as Bible teacher on a tour of Israel for Pastor Jamie and Life Church—the church she pastors in Williamstown, New Jersey. The tour was arranged by the Center for Holy Lands Studies. I fell in love with those precious congregation members! And I got to see this pastor in action, directing and encouraging, correcting and nurturing, teaching and protecting, proclaiming and praying. In all these roles, I saw Jamie being the shepherd—and how much her flock love her!

Since our first class together, I have had the joy of a second class with Pastor Jamie, this time in preaching. I have come full circle, from reading her outlines and sermons to now having watched her preach them in the pulpit. Everywhere, in all these roles, the same passion prevails.

As she shares her journey to ministry in this book, you will experience the amazing story that brings her to this place. You will come to know the trials, the testimonies, the burdens, the blessings, the broken places, and the healing that God brings.

Nothing is wasted! God is making beauty in them all. And this is why Jamie is so full of joy and passion. She knows that what God has done for her, God can also do for you!

—Deborah M. Gill, PhD
Professor, Biblical Studies and Exposition
Assemblies of God Theological Seminary,
Evangel University

INTRODUCTION

My journey to ministry appears like a labyrinth. While the destination remains known, the path to it isn't. Intricate passageways, high walls, seemingly dead ends, and back-to-the-start experiences fill my ministry labyrinth; but every inch is sacred. At times my journey through the labyrinth has felt like pure bliss, and at other times, like a crucible. I would have much preferred a ministry *pipeline* to a labyrinth; however, I wouldn't change a pen's stroke of my story.

"Miracle" is the only word that can explain my ministry journey. My life is comprised of one miracle after another. God has opened doors, parted rivers, and moved mountains on my behalf in order to fulfill His will for my life. Yet there has also been pain, hurt, betrayal, and discouragement. But with God, there is purpose even in pain. He has performed miracles throughout my journey both on top of the mountains and in the valleys.

This book is compiled into three parts: the story of my call to ministry, the story of my ministry journey, and the story of my future ministry.

I continue to write the latter part as I live it.

—Jamie Morgan

PART ONE

GOD CALLS ME TO MINISTRY

1

THE EARLY YEARS

I was born in Trenton, New Jersey, on November 8, 1963, to parents with good morals. As an only child, I received more love and attention than a child could ever want. And my parents insulated me from the evils of the outside world until I entered school; negative words and actions were completely foreign to me.

I remember wanting to have a relationship with God even when I was just a child. Occasionally, I cracked open and read the keepsake Bible that lay dusty on my nightstand. I often read the last chapter and slammed the Bible shut. The words in red, *"Yes,*

I am coming soon," (Rev. 22:20) confirmed my suspicions: if Jesus returned I wasn't ready.

I asked my parents to take me to church many times over the years. Each time, however, they explained that we weren't "the church-going kind of people." (Years later I had the honor of leading both of my parents to Jesus.)

Shame became a major theme in my life as it slowly developed and built in me through several bad experiences. I remember it first rearing its ugly head when I was still in kindergarten. It was the first week of school, and the class was playing outside during recess. When the teacher called us back into the classroom, I walked over to my chair and postured myself to sit; but instead, as I sat down I fell to the ground.

I looked up with tears in my eyes at a little boy standing over me. He had pulled the chair out from underneath me to get a laugh. His plan succeeded. I can still hear the laughter of my classmates and feel what I experienced that day—devastation, humiliation, and wanting to be invisible.

Many people would not find this incident particularly unusual; most would dismiss it as "kids will be kids," but not me. That event caused me early in life to make three damaging determinations: the first, the world is cruel; second, something must be wrong with me for someone to want to hurt me; and third, people cannot be trusted.

That public humiliation opened the door for the toxic emotion of shame to operate in my life.

The shame I'm talking about is to believe that one's being is flawed and that one is defective as a human being. This kind of shame is the greatest form of learned domestic violence there is. It destroys human life.[1]

The two greatest needs we have are the feelings of significance and security. Shame acts as a corrosive agent to strip these away—leaving us without dignity or hope. I believe there is no other emotion that better portrays hell than shame. It acts as a "demonic security blanket."[2]

I clutched my shame blanket for many years to come.

---

[1] John Bradshaw, *Healing of Shame* (Deerfield Beach, FL: Health Communications, Inc., 1988), pp. xvii-xviii.
[2] Melody D. Palm, "Embracing the Person of the Leader" (class notes for Core 3 Course at Assemblies of God Theological Seminary, Springfield, MO, 27 May 2016).

My first-grade teacher drove me deeper into shame. She humiliated me in front of the entire class. Public humiliation is just one of the causes of shame; but it is a strong cause. She conducted periodic "desk checks" to ensure our desks were neat and orderly. One day she surprised the class with a desk check. A sinking feeling began in my stomach. I was a sloppy child, and I knew my desk would reflect my messy ways.

The teacher approached my desk and peered inside it. She then instructed the class to make a wide circle and told me to stand in the middle. I did as ordered. She then picked up my desk, turned it upside down, and emptied the contents on the floor in the middle of the circle of my classmates. I was aghast. My belongings (dolls, report cards, school supplies, etc.) were strewn all over the floor for all to see.

With an angry tone, she addressed the class: "Do you see how Jamie keeps her desk? Don't ever, ever be like her!"

I stood, frozen and afraid to move, but at the same time I wanted to run as far away as possible. Research shows we experience guilt when we feel we have made a mistake; but we experience shame when we feel we *are* a mistake. And to me, the teacher announced to the class that I was a mistake. I went home that day too ashamed to tell my parents. What if they found out how horrible I was? For months I lived in fear that they would discover the "real" me.

The toxic emotion of shame compounded within me.

Shame continued to mount because of my family's financial woes. We were dirt poor. Many times we had nothing to eat but a loaf of bread, a jar of mustard, and a box of Kraft macaroni and cheese. I often went to school in the morning with a smile on my face and a growling stomach. At nine years old I volunteered to work in the school cafeteria in order to get a free lunch. I did that so my parents would have one less thing to worry about. At ten years old, I babysat so my family would have money for groceries.

I felt ashamed standing behind the cafeteria line with a hairnet on my head. And I felt ashamed to bring anyone into my home for fear they would see how I actually lived. I even felt ashamed when my friends complained about having pot roast for dinner. I longed for the day I could protest about having such a lavish meal.

I felt ashamed that I couldn't do anything about my parents' financial plight. And truly, that was way too much for a little girl to shoulder. I could feel anger beginning to mount up inside of me. As shame began to dominate me I began to lie to others about almost every area of my life—and also to myself. My lies and secrets were making me emotionally sick. And as I grew in age, I also grew in shame.

Academically, my parents expected me to be the best and brightest child in the room.

"Was there anyone who scored higher than you?" "Did anyone get a trophy bigger than yours?" "What is wrong with your teacher that she did not select you for the role?" Those were typical of the questions my parents asked.

Lesson learned: Don't let someone else's bondages become yours.

When I reached the seventh grade, I had cystic acne—the most severe kind. There wasn't a spot on my face that did not have a pustule. Many called me "zit face" or "pimple face." I was at an age when girls want boys to like them. I was no exception. But one day a boy spoke to me and jeered, "You would be pretty if they put a bag over your head!"

I was ashamed with how I looked.

The acne persisted throughout my high school years and into young adulthood. While acne is hardly unusual, and is a normal part of being a teen-ager, for me it was devastating. It became one more thing that confirmed to me that I was defective. It caused me to withdraw socially and isolate myself from others. But I stopped caring. I no longer strived to be the best in my class, and I worked even harder at being invisible.

Isolation is a by-product of shame.

It was like I had a running tape recorder playing in my head. And I now understand that also was a result of shame. The tape recorder in my head shouted, "No one wants to hear what you have to say."

That recording played over and over and it dominated my thought life. Looking back now, I believe the devil knew I was called to be a minister of the Gospel, and he knew there would come a day when many would need to hear what God has to say through me. So he used *shame* like a demonic duct tape to cover my mouth to keep me quiet and in my place.

When I was fifteen years old, my family moved from Pennsylvania to New Jersey. I was the new girl in school, and I befriended anyone who would let me. I began making poor relationship decisions because of my desperation for friends. I started attending parties on the weekends, and the more I partied the more my grades started slipping. I began to drink with my friends. I liked the high that alcohol gave me, but more than that, I enjoyed its numbing qualities. Alcohol placed a temporary bandage on my emotional pain.

I became an extrovert when I drank. I became more like the person I yearned to be as the alcohol and the "fun" I was having with my partying friends masked my emotional pain. It felt good to be loose and "free." The more I drank, the "freer" I became. My drinking increased—always with the goal of drunkenness.

By the time I was a young adult, I drank from morning until night. And that damaging pattern continued into my twenties.

I married at the age of twenty-two, and a year later I found out I was expecting. I wanted a healthy baby, so I actually gave up drinking during the pregnancy. However, I began to drink again after I gave birth to a beautiful baby boy. In fact, when my friends visited me in the hospital, I instructed them to bring me a bottle of alcohol instead of flowers. I sipped Baileys Irish Cream while the nurses weren't looking.

In addition to being an alcoholic I also began having panic attacks. My first anxiety attack happened at work. I thought I was dying, so I had a coworker drive me to the hospital. Before long I began having panic attacks while driving, at the post office, at the bank, at the grocery store—everywhere.

I then began withdrawing in a serious way. My world became smaller and smaller. Within a month, I was agoraphobic,[3] and I became a prisoner in my own home. The doctor prescribed Xanax for my anxiety. And I self-prescribed cocktails of Xanax and alcohol.

---

[3] Agoraphobia—an abnormal fear of being in crowds, public places, or open areas.

I became severely depressed. I was lying in bed with the covers pulled up over my head many times when my husband left for work in the morning. And many times when he returned in the evening he found me still there in the same position. I experienced anxiety attacks day and night. My entire world eventually became limited to my bed.

Anger turned inward leads to depression.

My life was a vicious cycle of shame, pain, fear, and depression; shame, pain, fear, and depression—a cycle that revolved over and over again. My entire existence was defined by a never-ending sequence of dangerous emotions that were leading me to destruction. The only temporary reprieve I had was when I was in a drunken state.

But the cycle began to break the day I met the Lord Jesus Christ.

Questions for Reflection – Chapter 1

1. What helped you from this chapter? What gave you a different perspective? What surprised you the most?

_____

_____

_____

_____

_____

_____

2. Read and meditate on Jeremiah 1:4-5, Jeremiah 29:11, and Ephesians 5:15. Share what you feel God is revealing to you through these passages.

_____

_____

_____

_____

_____

3. Emotional pain takes many forms. What emotional baggage do you continue to drag around from your past?

_____

_____

_____

_____

_____

_____

_____

_____

4. What hurtful words were spoken that deeply wounded you?

_____

_____

_____

_____

_____

_____

_____

5. Is there a running tape recorder (lies of the enemy) that plays over and over in your head? What does the recording (enemy) say?

_____

_____

_____

_____

_____

_____

_____

_____

6. Comparison is a trap of the enemy. In what areas do you compare yourself with others?

_____

_____

_____

_____

_____

_____

_____

_____

7. We have all been wounded and need healing. A "wounded healer," however, is someone who ministers while still in emotional pain; a "wounded healer" bleeds on the person to whom they minister. Describe a scenario when this might occur.

_____

_____

_____

_____

_____

_____

_____

8. Our past must be healed in order to effectively minister in the future. How have past hurts and words inhibited you from fully answering the call on your life?

_____

_____

_____

_____

_____

_____

9. To conquer these types of bondages we must become intentional. What is your plan to gain victory over these strongholds?

_____

_____

_____

_____

_____

_____

_____

_____

10. Describe your first recollection of desiring a relationship with God. How old were you and what was going on in your life?

_____

_____

_____

_____

_____

_____

_____

_____

11. What is the definition of *trailblazer*? Look it up in the dictionary and write the definition here:

_____

_____

_____

_____

_____

_____

_____

_____

_____

2

My Savior Was Calling

"Lord, I ask You to take this messed up girl; and if You can do anything with her life, I ask You to do it. I will go wherever You ask me to go, do whatever You ask me to do, and say whatever You ask me to say. I am Yours."

This was my prayer when I gave my life to the Lord on December 26, 1989, in the back bedroom of the home where I lived with my husband and young son. At twenty-six years of age, I had come to the end of myself. I was a raging alcoholic, an agoraphobic, and severely depressed. I had failed at life, and I stood in need of a Savior.

My depression and despondency always heightened after the sun went down, and that night, the day after Christmas, was no different; it was dreadful. But with that prayer, the course of my life changed forever.

Falling to my knees next to my bed, I began weeping. I looked up at the dark New Jersey sky and prayed, "God, I don't know anything about You. But I believe You are real, and that You created me. And I believe Your plans for my life have got to be better than what I am living."

Jesus revealed Himself to me as Lord and Savior during this desperate appeal. I gave my life to Him, and when I stood to my feet, the chains of alcohol addiction, fear, and depression miraculously shattered.

Freedom has a name. His name is Jesus.

Then I had an encounter with the Holy Spirit two years later. I had been frequenting a Christian bookstore in my town. Each time I went in, the owner shared with me something about the baptism in the Holy Spirit. My response was always the same: That experience is not for today. I was parroting what the church I attended at the time believed.

However, she relentlessly insisted I needed that baptism. And she was right.

One day, after she brought the subject up yet again, she handed me a book. It was *The Real Faith* by Kenneth E. Hagin. The book was about receiving, by faith, whatever a person needed from God. I took it home and immediately began reading. The author shared Scriptures that clearly pointed to the truth that the baptism in the Holy Spirit was for today. And eventually I was convinced.

The only thing I knew for sure at that time was that I wanted everything God had for me. So I fell to my knees in prayer—again at my bedside—and I asked God for the baptism in the Holy Spirit.

I said, "Lord, if the baptism in the Holy Spirit is from You, I want it. I receive it now by faith. I want everything You have for me."

I stood up and began thanking God for it. As I was praising God, a light and heat, like I had never before experienced, flooded the upstairs bedroom of our small Cape Cod-style house. It was like someone turned on a stadium lamp that shone through my bedroom window. My praise in English then turned into my own personal, spiritual prayer language.

And my Christian walk has never been the same.

My thirties constituted my "decade of healing." I was thoroughly discipled; I learned how to walk by faith and walk in love; and my mind was renewed by God's Word. I also got my priorities in order. The lifelong process of sanctification had begun in me. I had been instantly delivered from substance abuse, fear, and depression, but my freedom from shame and insecurity came only as I grew as a Christian and walked out those things one step at a time.

My self-esteem had plummeted lower than low, but that soon began to change. I began to realize that whatever self-worth I previously had was based upon my parents' opinion. And I came to understand that no matter how positive or affirming it seemed, it was all built on shifting sand.

I learned more and more about Jesus, our solid Rock.[4] I found out it was on the Rock of Christ Jesus upon which we should build our lives—our spiritual

---

[4] "For I do not want you to be ignorant of the fact, brothers, that our forefathers were all under the cloud and that they all passed through the sea. They were all baptized into Moses in the cloud and in the sea. They all ate the same spiritual food and drank the same

house—not sand.[5] Rock is solid; sand is not. I wanted my life to stand in the storm, so I searched the Scriptures for who I was in Christ, and more importantly, who Christ was in me.

I purchased index cards and wrote down every verse I could find in the Bible that contains the phrases *in Him, because of Jesus,* and *through Him.* I read those verses out loud three times a day—for months and months and months. I took God's Word like medicine.

I then used a cassette tape recorder to record myself reading those verses. I placed the recorder under my bed and listened to the recording as I slept. I spoke the Scriptures when my insecurity and shame began to ease, and I recited them when it got

spiritual drink; for they drank from the spiritual rock that accompanied them, and that rock was Christ" (1 Corinthians 10:1-4).

[5] "I will show you what he is like who comes to me and hears my words and puts them into practice. He is like a man building a house, who dug down deep and laid the foundation on rock. When a flood came, the torrent struck that house but could not shake it, because it was well built. But the one who hears my words and does not put them into practice is like a man who built a house on the ground without a foundation. The moment the torrent struck that house, it collapsed and its destruction was complete.

"He is like a man building a house, who dug down deep and laid the foundation on rock. When a flood came, the torrent struck that house but could not shake it, because it was well built" (Luke 6:47-48).

worse. I became tired of hearing my own voice, but verse by verse, my identity in Christ was being built on the Rock.

On the way to finding out who I am in Christ I received and came to understand God's extravagant gift of grace. And because of that, I was healed and delivered from the awful sense of shame that once ruled my life. As a result of what Jesus *did* for me, and because of what the Holy Spirit did *within* me, I was both empowered and enabled to permanently hit the stop button on the "tape recorder of shame."

Questions for Reflection – Chapter 2

1. What helped you from this chapter? What gave you a different perspective? What surprised you the most?

_____

_____

_____

_____

_____

_____

_____

_____

2. Briefly describe your salvation experience. How did God encounter you?

_____

_____

_____

_____

_____

_____

_____

_____

3. Jesus told the disciples to wait in Jerusalem until they were empowered by the Holy Spirit (Acts 1:1-9). As impassioned as they were to spread the Gospel, Jesus didn't want them to begin their ministries until they were baptized in the Holy Spirit. It was the last thing Jesus said before He ascended into heaven. Why do you think He gave the disciples this instruction?

_____

_____

_____

_____

_____

_____

_____

_____

_____

_____

_____

_____

_____

_____

_____

4. Describe what happened when you were baptized in the Holy Spirit.

_____

_____

_____

_____

_____

_____

_____

_____

5. Describe what transpires when we pray in our prayer language every day. Do you think this is crucial to the fulfillment of your call?

_____

_____

_____

_____

_____

_____

_____

_____

6. It is crucial we know who we are in Christ. List Scriptures that speak of your identity in Christ in areas that you still need to gain victory.

_____

_____

_____

_____

_____

_____

_____

7. It is paramount to speak God's Word about ourselves and every situation in life. Give an example of how not doing this could thwart the call on your life.

_____

_____

_____

_____

_____

_____

_____

8. Christian leaders who have built their lives on the Rock of Christ Jesus lead from a place of peace, no matter the circumstances. This is of utmost importance in the ministry. When trials come, how do you typically react?

_____

_____

_____

_____

_____

_____

_____

_____

_____

_____

_____

_____

_____

_____

_____

_____

_____

_____

_____

9. God's gift of extravagant grace is available for every difficult situation in life—including the ministry. God freely provides His grace, however, we must learn how to walk in that grace. What might it look like when someone in the ministry walks in the grace that God freely gives? What does it look like when someone does not?

_____

_____

_____

_____

_____

_____

_____

_____

_____

_____

_____

_____

_____

_____

_____

_____

10. Describe the healing process you experienced or the healing that you still need. If you are still in need of healing, what plan do you have in place to cooperate with God's healing power?

_____

_____

_____

_____

_____

_____

_____

_____

_____

_____

_____

_____

_____

_____

_____

_____

_____

11. The biggest black eye we give the devil, and more importantly the most glory we can give to God, is to allow God to heal us and then through our testimony, bring salvation and healing to others. Describe the aspects of your testimony that can bring salvation and healing to others.

_____

_____

_____

_____

_____

_____

_____

_____

_____

_____

_____

_____

_____

_____

_____

_____

_____

_____

3

Signposts for My Calling

Some people receive their calling to ministry gradually and progressively, yet others experience an abrupt and dramatic *call encounter*. My calling to ministry came as a combination of both. One of the keys to my call discovery was to persistently seek God regarding it.

Believers will find their calling when they seek it.

We need to seek our calling like a gold miner digging for gold. Sometimes a miner will dig for a long time before the gold appears before him. So pursuing our callings can require patience and faith.

But when gold is discovered, the gold miner digs excitedly as he follows the glimmer he sees on the wall of the mine shaft. God will typically give us a glimpse of our calling, and then another glimpse, and so on, until we find our calling and continually walk in the light He has given us.

As I grew in my Christian faith, I prayed daily and practiced all manner of intercession. But there were seven prayers that were foundational to my calling coming to fruition:

1. What is my purpose in life?
2. Anoint me for what I am called to do.
3. Give me wisdom and discernment.
4. Root out all selfishness and pride from my life.
5. Give me a vast harvest of souls.
6. Expose what needs to be exposed and reveal what needs to be revealed.
7. Increase my pain threshold.

Unquestionably, Christians seldom utter the prayer, "Increase my pain threshold," but it remains crucial to the fulfillment of the callings God places on our lives. Christians will grow and mature only to the level of their pain threshold. If they draw a line in the sand and say, "No more pain!" they will stymie both their personal and ministry growth.

I found an essential element in my ability to discover my calling while serving my church. I learned that the local church houses God's plan for growth in our lives. If the pastor asked me to make phone calls, I placed calls like I was calling Jesus. If the pastor's wife needed my help to clean the church, I swept the floors like I was sweeping the streets of gold. And as I served in so many, sometimes mundane ways, my gifts and talents began to emerge like signposts pointing in the direction of God's ordained destiny for my life.

Then eventually, as I conducted a women's midweek Bible study, my teaching and preaching gifts emerged. As I hosted what we called a *cell group*, shepherding gifts surfaced. As I spearheaded church outreaches, my calling as evangelist developed. And as I led other ministries, various leadership gifts began to appear. Most importantly, however, through all of those experiences God cultivated within me a servant's heart needed for full-time ministry.

God also loudly proclaimed His call to me by using pain and conflict that came my way while I was doing His business. When God instructed me to speak at my father's funeral, I learned obedience at all costs. When He asked me to serve in a ministry completely outside of my skill set, I learned to wholly rely on Him. When I battled Lyme disease for fifteen long years, I developed an unrelenting perseverance and unwavering faith while standing on God's Word for my healing. I struggled with all those things, but in each of my struggles God used what the devil wanted to use for my harm and turned it around for my good.

Likewise, when I was employed at a job that under most circumstances I would never have chosen, I learned how to die to *self*. When I received criticism from those closest to me, I learned to stand fixed and immovable—prepared for the day when I would receive criticism from the body of Christ at large. When I excitedly received my first speaking invitation, only to find out the women's retreat had been cancelled and the host forgot to tell me, I learned the much-needed ministry skill of encouraging oneself in the Lord. And when I was given a budget of twenty-five dollars to conduct a weeklong vacation school for the children in the community, I learned to pray, believe, and receive the financial provision needed to conduct an effective outreach.

God doesn't waste pain.

Learning to receive correction without taking offense was also an immense portion of my preparation for ministry. And the amount and kind of correction I received actually served to point to the vast call that was on my life. God is so good! In the moment of pain, although I didn't connect the dots, my loving heavenly Father revealed that the pain I felt was proof of His call on my life, too.

Paul told Timothy to "*. . . correct, rebuke and encourage—with great patience and careful instruction*"[6] those to whom he ministered. Two-thirds of Paul's instructions to young Pastor Timothy were less than encouraging as Paul counseled Timothy on the trouble and painful things that Timothy had to confront as a leader.

My pastor taught me a myriad of things needed for success in ministry. Among them were walking by faith, receiving from God, speaking the Word,

---

[6] 2 Timothy 4:2.

walking in love; and there was much more. However, one of the greatest gifts he gave to me was correction. Many years later, during my ordination ceremony, I was able to thank my pastor for that gift.

As my pastor stood opposite of me at the ordination ceremony and placed the stole of ministry around my neck (representing the *mantle* of ministry), tears began to flow down my cheeks. I said to him, "Thank you for all of your words of correction. Without them I would not be standing here today."

In that moment, of all the many things he had taught me, it was his correction for which I was most grateful. In my journey toward my calling, God used many different signposts to point me toward it, and correction and pain were among them. All the time spent in the days of preparation that the Holy Spirit faithfully leads us through, including the days of suffering pain, is never lost time.

All the signposts are installed along the way to direct us in our journey, and they all are vital to our future success in ministry.

Questions for Reflection – Chapter 3

1. What helped you from this chapter? What gave you a different perspective? What surprised you the most?

_____

_____

_____

_____

_____

_____

_____

2. One of the greatest joys in life is walking in the call of God; however, some of the deepest pain occurs when you are fulfilling your purpose. List the types of pain that accompany ministry.

_____

_____

_____

_____

_____

_____

3. Describe your pain tolerance (emotional, spiritual, and physical) and ways you can increase your pain threshold.

_____

_____

_____

_____

_____

_____

_____

_____

4. Taking offense when hurt, slighted, or overlooked is a trap of the enemy. Honestly describe how you respond when the enemy dangles the temptation of offense in front of you.

_____

_____

_____

_____

_____

_____

_____

_____

5. Feedback is the breakfast of champions. Why is the ability to receive correction important to fulfilling your call?

_____

_____

_____

_____

_____

_____

_____

_____

_____

6. How can you develop an attitude of gratitude regarding correction?

_____

_____

_____

_____

_____

_____

_____

_____

7. The local church is the growth plan for the Christian and the launching pad for our call. "The righteous will flourish like a palm tree, they will grow like a cedar of Lebanon; *planted in the house of the Lord*" (Psalm 92:12-13, emphasis added). How have you planted yourself in your local church? How can you more deeply root yourself?

_____

_____

_____

_____

_____

_____

_____

_____

_____

_____

_____

_____

_____

_____

_____

_____

_____

8. A servant's heart is the willingness to do anything God asks with a good attitude. Many Christians say, "Jesus, I'll do anything for You!" yet fail to do what He is asking them. Others will do what He asks, but will complain while they are doing it. List the ways you can cultivate a servant's heart.

_____

_____

_____

_____

_____

_____

_____

_____

_____

_____

_____

_____

_____

_____

_____

_____

9. God gives us glimpses or signposts pointing to our calling. They help us head in the direction of our purpose. Answer the following "signposts" questions:

a. What do you love to do? Often what we love to do reveals our purpose in life.

_____

_____

_____

_____

_____

_____

_____

_____

_____

_____

_____

_____

_____

_____

_____

_____

_____

_____

b. What makes me angry? Anger is passion that can be a signal that we are called to correct something.

_____

_____

_____

_____

_____

_____

_____

_____

c. What makes me cry? Sorrow can reveal what we are called to heal.

_____

_____

_____

_____

_____

_____

_____

_____

4

My Official Call Encounter

It was in September 1999, ten years after my salvation, when God officially called me into the ministry. One morning, as I sat in a recliner conducting my usual morning devotions, the Lord's presence flooded my living room.

God proclaimed, "You have been called and chosen to evangelize the nations."

I was overjoyed and shocked all at the same time.

A plethora of questions flooded my mind: "How do I start?" "Where will I get the needed finances?"

Although I did not receive immediate answers to my questions, I rejoiced that God had officially called me. I remained entirely devoted to following Him. I was undaunted by the unanswered questions. I was fully prepared to do anything He required.

That period of my ministry journey was what I refer to as the time I felt pregnant with the call of God. When a newly pregnant woman announces she is pregnant, she doesn't look pregnant. That was how I felt. God had called me, but my life showed little evidence, and the people around me could not see it.

When I told others about my ministry calling, I naively thought they would be happy for me. But while a handful of my friends did encourage me, I received little support from most. That included several friends from whom the Lord over time instructed me to distance myself. Their opinions mattered to me; remaining too close to them would have hampered my call.

I questioned how I could pursue my calling with so little support from the people around me. But I continued to prepare myself for my new mission. I sent for information from the Berean School of the Bible (BSB)—the Assemblies of God online school for ministry preparation. I poured over the catalog of classes and studies with great excitement in my heart. However, two details stopped me from moving forward. There was the matter of the $1,500 tuition, and there was my need to feel the assurance that enrolling in the school was God's will for me.

Soon after that, I sat at lunch with a godly coworker whom I greatly respected. As we ate, I casually mentioned that I was praying about taking Bible courses. He responded, "Jamie, there are just some things that you don't have to pray about. You are called to the ministry! Enroll in that Bible school!"

As he spoke these words, I could feel the presence of God speaking through him. I marvel how that one conversation forever changed the course of my life. I felt so inspired and full of faith that I went home, enrolled, and ordered material from BSB.

I had no idea at the time how I was going to pay for the material, but I decided to trust God for it. And a few weeks after receiving the material, I received an unexpected envelope in the mail from a family in our church. Inside the envelope was a check for $1,500 accompanied by a note. The enclosed note read: "We want to sow into your future ministry."

The miracles God has performed for my finances over the years still amazes me.

After I completed the Berean courses, I applied for the first level of ministerial credentialing. I needed three friends to answer questions about my character, my calling, and my fitness for ministry. I identified the three friends and mailed a reference form to each of them.

A few days later, one of those friends called me. She stammered around, but finally said, "I'm sorry, Jamie, I can't give you a reference . . . I don't believe that women are called to be ministers."

I was deeply hurt by that response. She was a trusted friend, who in the past had given me her full support in what I had done in the church, and to whom I had greatly ministered. I was her cell group leader, had visited her in the hospital, had shared the Gospel with her unsaved husband, had cooked her meals when she was sick, had counseled her when she was in emotional duress—God had used me to shepherd her. I was floored by this surprise attack! I was also rattled by that experience because never before had I needed to defend my calling.

If you don't get bitter you'll make it!

I have discovered over my years of ministry that there are two particular types of people who exist to affect our future, and who are sometimes not recognized for their potential to impact our lives. There are the *dream-encouragers*, and there are the *dream-stealers*. The dream-encouragers are of course the most positive people with whom to surround yourself; but unfortunately they are sometimes the hardest ones to find. The dream-stealers do exactly what the title of their group implies, and they sometimes surround you as unwanted mosquitos.

But regardless of how we feel about either group, the truth is, there is something to be gained by dealing with both dream-encouragers and dream-stealers. You see, we have a wonderful God and Savior who will use both types of people to give us greater resolve and propel us forward. God sends people into our lives, and the devil sends people into our lives, but God uses all of them to mold and shape us as we come to understand and respond to our call encounters.

Questions for Reflection – Chapter 4

1. What helped you from this chapter? What gave you a different perspective? What surprised you the most?

_____

_____

_____

_____

_____

_____

_____

_____

2. What has God spoken to you regarding your purpose(s) in life?

_____

_____

_____

_____

_____

_____

_____

_____

3. Our ministry call is sacred and precious; we should use wisdom with whom we share it. "Do not give dogs what is sacred; do not throw your pearls to pigs. If you do, they may trample them under their feet, and turn and tear you to pieces" (Matt. 7:6). If you have been confronted by a dream-stealer, how did you respond?

_____

_____

_____

_____

_____

_____

_____

_____

_____

_____

_____

_____

_____

_____

_____

_____

4. Take time to identify the dream-encouragers and dream-stealers in your life. How are both of these affecting your call? Are there people you need to distance yourself from, no matter how difficult, in order to see your call come to pass?

_____

_____

_____

_____

_____

_____

_____

_____

_____

_____

_____

_____

_____

_____

_____

_____

_____

5. Discouragement means "no courage to continue." Often discouragement will attack when the people around us don't give the encouragement we need. Self-pity will lead to discouragement every time! But let's face it—no one will be as excited about your dream from God, than you. Practically speaking, how do you encourage yourself in the Lord when there is resistance or little to no encouragement?

_____

_____

_____

_____

_____

_____

_____

_____

_____

_____

_____

_____

_____

_____

6. Another area of discouragement comes when the enemy reminds us of our past failures. Most of us could write a book on our mistakes, flops, wash-outs, mess-ups, botches, duds, and failures. We've all started projects we didn't finish, wasted both time and money, said things we shouldn't have said, and done things we shouldn't have done. The enemy will remind us of our past failures in order to prevent us from answering God's call on our lives. But when driving down the highway of life, rip off the rear-view mirror! What Scripture verse(s) can you stand on when the enemy attacks in this manner?

_____

_____

_____

_____

_____

_____

_____

_____

_____

_____

_____

7. Read and meditate on James 1:2-4. Resiliency is the ability to bounce back from negative circumstances. Perseverant faith in times of trial produces spiritual maturity and resiliency. How does God use both dream-encouragers and dream-stealers to give us Holy Spirit resiliency?

_____

_____

_____

_____

_____

_____

_____

_____

_____

_____

_____

_____

_____

_____

_____

_____

8. Betrayal is one of the deepest hurts in ministry and one that almost everyone who answers God's call experiences sometime in their lives. If it happens to you, how will you respond?

_____

_____

_____

_____

_____

_____

_____

_____

9. What steps have you taken to prepare for your calling?

_____

_____

_____

_____

_____

_____

_____

_____

_____

10. God pays for what He orders; He equips whom He calls. Share a time when God miraculously provided for your needs.

_____

_____

_____

_____

_____

_____

_____

_____

_____

_____

_____

_____

_____

_____

_____

_____

_____

_____

_____

_____

5

DEFENDING MY CALLING

Even as I prepared to receive my credentials as a minister of the Gospel, I had to formulate a personal theology of women in ministry. A kaleidoscope is a cylinder that uses two mirrors to reflect pieces of glass. This two-mirror system creates polychromatic patterns. The mirrors display the same patterns repeated endlessly. First Corinthians 14:34-35 and 1 Timothy 2:11-12 constitute the two-mirror system through which many Christians view the topic of women in ministry.[7] This results in

---

[7] All Scripture quotations, unless otherwise noted, are from the New International Version.

a patterned, constricted, and skewed interpretation of these verses.[8]

Looking at the topic of women in ministry through just these two verses would be like going to a huge amusement park, visiting only the hot dog stand and the stroller rental, but saying you have a thorough knowledge of the entire park. The whole counsel of God, from Genesis to Revelation, needs to be taken into consideration regarding any topic in the Bible—including the subject of women in ministry.

This two-passage view, versus the whole counsel of God, prohibits countless women from pastoring churches, becoming board members, and preaching sermons. The incorrect interpretations of these two verses have frustrated and diminished the gifts, talents, and mantles of women called to biblical leadership. Because of the mishandling of Scripture, the enemy has been able to silence the mouths of many women to prevent them from participating in the Great Commission.

---

[8] Richard Clark Kroeger and Catherine Clark Kroeger, *I Suffer Not a Woman* (Grand Rapids, MI: Baker Books, 2003), 12.

Because of erroneous interpretations of the Bible, the Old Testament examples of women like Huldah, Deborah, and Miriam are often disregarded, while the ministries of New Testament women such as Priscilla, Phoebe, and Junia remain largely overlooked.[9] The only antidote for these injustices resides in discovering Paul's original intent when he penned those words to the Corinthian believers, and to Timothy and his flock in Ephesus, for dealing with "isolated issues that troubled these two specific congregations."[10]

As people look through the kaleidoscope they see what the first mirror displays:

Women should remain silent in the churches. They are not allowed to speak, but must be in submission, as the law says. If they want to inquire about something, they should ask their own husbands at home; for it is disgraceful for a woman to speak in the church.

—1 Cor. 14:34-35

---

[9] Gordon D. Fee and Douglas Stuart, *How to Read the Bible for All Its Worth* (Grand Rapids, MI: Zondervan, 2003), p. 28.

[10] Gordon D. Fee and Douglas Stuart, *How to Read the Bible for All Its Worth* (Grand Rapids, MI: Zondervan, 2003), p. 28.

In this passage, Paul addresses a specific group of women who kept disrupting the service by asking inconsequential questions.[11] The universal application from this passage remains this: "Do not exercise your freedoms at the expense of others."[12] An example of a specific application might be: "Students who did not do their homework should not ask silly questions in class."[13]

Furthermore, in the same chapter of 1 Corinthians the apostle Paul instructs a group of people to "be silent" in two other separate situations: those who speak in tongues (v. 28), and those who prophesy (v. 30).[14] It is apparent that "Paul's 'be silent' admonition was not an 'absolutely-forever-under-every-circumstance-and-at-all-times' injunction against those who spoke in tongues, prophesied, or women."[15]

---

[11] Craig S. Keener, *Paul, Women and Wives* (Grand Rapids, MI: Baker Academic, 1992), p. 17.

[12] Deborah M. Gill, "Biblical Theology of Women in Leadership" (class notes for Core 2 Course at Assemblies of God Theological Seminary, Springfield, MO, February 23, 2016).

[13] Craig S. Keener, *Paul, Women and Wives* (Grand Rapids, MI: Baker Academic, 1992), p . 88.

[14] Deborah M. Gill and Barbara Cavaness, *God's Women Then and Now* (Colorado Springs: Authentic Books, 2009), p. 127.

[15] Loren Cunningham and David Joel Hamilton, *Why Not Women?* (Seattle: Youth with a Mission Publishing, 2000), p. 96.

Paul instructed the women that "we want you to learn, but not at the expense of others."[16]

Then, as people continue to peer into the kaleidoscope, the second mirror displays this:

A woman should learn in quietness and full submission. I do not permit a woman to teach or to assume authority over a man; she must be quiet.   —1 Tim. 2:11-12

In this passage Paul was addressing a specific group of women who were presenting erroneous teaching.[17] The universal principle in this passage is that "Paul didn't make women taboo; he made chaos and heresy taboo."[18] Today's application is that order needs to be kept in the Church in order for biblical discipleship to take place.[19]

I highly suggest that all people who are called into the ministry, male or female, formulate a

---

[16] Deborah M. Gill, *Biblical Theology of Women in Leadership*.

[17] Craig S. Keener, *Paul, Women and Wives* (Grand Rapids, MI: Baker Academic, 1992), p. 108.

[18] Loren Cunningham and David Joel Hamilton, *Why Not Women?* (Seattle: Youth with a Mission Publishing, 2000), p. 203.

[19] Deborah M. Gill and Barbara Cavaness, *God's Women Then and Now* (Colorado Springs: Authentic Books, 2009), p. 158.

ministry confession—a one-minute elevator speech that briefly articulates their calling. They should review it often, every day if they need to, in order to intentionally remind themselves of the call of God on their lives. I did exactly that, and when I first started in the ministry, I read it out loud to myself before every service in which I ministered. I also read it when the devil tried to tell me I wasn't called, or when discouragement tried to set in.

Here is my ministry confession:

I am called by God to be a minister of the Gospel. He has anointed me, appointed me, and equipped me, for such a time as this to fulfill the Great Commission.
(Matthew 22:3-39; Luke 4:18; Hebrews 13:21; Mathew 28:16-20)

I stand firm in my call.

I have been given a mandate from God to be a pastor in His Church, preach the Gospel, win the lost, lay hands on the sick, cast out demons, fan the flame of revival, and call the

Church back to the place of prayer and evangelism—all of which I do with great boldness and without hindrance.

(Ephesians. 4:11-13; Mark 16:15-18;
Acts 28:31; Matthew 21:13).

I stand firm in my call.

My feet are beautiful, my words are full of power, my mind is filled with wisdom, my eyes are fixed on Jesus, and my hand is to the plow.

(Romans 10:15; Luke 21:15; James 1:5-8;
Hebrews 12:2; Luke 9:62).

I stand firm in my call.

I am a daughter of God, upon whom He has poured His Spirit. God chooses whom He chooses—and He has chosen me.

(Acts 2:16-21; 1 Samuel 16:7,
Galatians 3:38).

I stand firm in my call.

Despite setbacks and discouragements, God has always placed mentors in my life to encourage me as a woman in ministry. My mentors have included women ministers of the past such as Maria Woodworth-Etter, Aimee Semple McPherson, Katherine Kuhlman, and Catherine Booth. Although long gone, these sisters cheered me on from the pages of their biographies to pursue my calling. The devil is the devil no matter what decade we live in. And decades after their personal ministries on earth ended, God used their stories of perseverance in ministry to spur me on to good works.

Questions for Reflection – Chapter 5

1. What helped you from this chapter? What gave you a different perspective? What surprised you the most?

_____

_____

_____

_____

_____

_____

_____

_____

2. Which Bible characters most inspire you in the quest to fulfill your purpose?

_____

_____

_____

_____

_____

_____

_____

_____

3. Which people from Christian history have brought you the most inspiration?

_____

_____

_____

_____

_____

_____

_____

_____

_____

_____

_____

_____

_____

_____

_____

_____

_____

_____

_____

_____

4. Imagine you had only sixty seconds (e.g., ascending an elevator) to share your call to ministry. What would you say? What scriptural proof would you give to support your call? Share you sixty-second elevator speech here:

_____

_____

_____

_____

_____

_____

_____

_____

_____

_____

_____

_____

_____

_____

_____

_____

_____

_____

PART TWO

MY MINISTRY JOURNEY

6

THE MINISTRY OF EVANGELISM

My life's verse:

He [Paul] proclaimed the kingdom of God and taught about the Lord Jesus Christ—with all boldness and without hindrance. —Acts 28:31

I have always had a passion for souls. From the moment of my salvation, I could feel God's heartbeat—souls, souls, souls. And that feeling only grew stronger as I answered God's call. The first ministry to which I applied myself after receiving my calling was the ministry of evangelism.

I led the evangelism and discipleship ministries of my local church. I piloted soul-winning outreaches. I taught the people of my cell group how to witness, and together we went on small-group evangelism excursions. I hosted a shortwave radio program to encourage missionaries around the world in their soul-winning efforts. I also wrote an evangelism-training curriculum that I named *Here I Am: Send Me,* and I conducted one-day evangelism seminars for other churches in my region.

I also had a passion to see new believers thoroughly discipled. I wrote an eight-week curriculum to establish new Christians in their walk with the Lord and taught those who were mature in their faith how to mentor them. I matched new believers with personal mentors, monitored their progress, and reported their growth to my pastor. I even had several articles published in *Discipleship Journal.*[20] I stayed busy building the Kingdom. It was pure joy.

If you cut me, I bleed evangelism. In those days I even clipped pictures from articles about Reinhard Bonnke's African crusades and would cry out to

---

[20] *Discipleship Journal*—published since 1981 by the Navigators.

God for souls. I sought and consumed all manner of encouragement and inspiration for my ministry.

I was attending a women's retreat in March 2002, when a speaker prophesied of the ministry to which I was called. Through her words, God graciously afforded me a glimpse into my future ministry.

As the speaker prayed for me, she bent down, anointed my shins with oil, and proclaimed:

"I see your legs like tree trunks. I have seen other people's feet firmly planted as I have prayed for them, but never the entire leg planted. You are solid, not fragile, not easily tripped or offended. God has given you leadership legs because you are called to leadership, and tree-trunk legs are to enable you to stand in His call."

She then inquired if I was a minister. I told her that I wasn't, and she proceeded to pour the entire bottle of anointing oil over my head. It began dripping down my hair onto my face and eyes.

"God has called you to be a teacher of the Word," she continued, "but He has also called you to be a pastor. You have a pastor-teacher calling."

She repeated this several times and then called me "Reverend Jamie."

I was elated! My calling to ministry had finally been confirmed! Now nothing could stand in my way—or so I thought.

I submit any directional prophetic word I receive to the authority of someone I look to for leadership. I always desire to receive wise counsel. Therefore, the Monday after the retreat, I did just that.

"No," my ministry leader responded, "women are not called to be pastors."

Then he proceeded to give me one example after the next of female senior pastors who were hugely unsuccessful in the ministry. I sat speechless.

"If women were supposed to be ministers," the leader continued, "Jesus would have chosen at least one female apostle among the twelve."

If I had understood things then as I do now, I would have countered that Jesus *did*, in fact, choose twelve men—*and* they were all Jewish. If Jesus precluded women from ministry, then all *gentile men* would have been excluded from ministry as well.[21] I would have continued by demonstrating from the Bible that both women and gentile men held leadership positions in the early Church after the twelve began their ministries; therefore, women and gentiles can also serve in biblical leadership roles today.[22]

Furthermore, I would have explained that Jesus was groundbreaking in His inclusiveness of women, both in rhetoric and treatment. Jesus reached out to, and cared for, both genders equally. He taught women, included them in doctrinal discourses and parables, and incorporated them into His larger group of disciples. Jesus did all of this in a cultural climate in which there was severe discrimination and mistreatment of women.[23] In those days men didn't even publicly acknowledge women when entering a room.[24]

Similarly, I would have made the strong point that both genders have shared origins, as well as common destinies. The origins of both man and woman

---

[21] Deborah M. Gill, *Biblical Theology of Women in Leadership*.

[22] Deborah M. Gill, *The Biblical Liberated Woman*, Paraclete 29 (1995), p. 9.

[23] Deborah M. Gill and Barbara Cavaness, *God's Women Then and Now* (Colorado Springs: Authentic Books, 2009), pp. 73-82.

[24] Deborah M. Gill, *Biblical Theology of Women in Leadership*.

became inseparably connected during creation. And they fell together when they disobeyed God in the garden. Because of these two things, their destinies are also forever linked. They are both, in the same exact way, lost in sin and in need of the Redeemer.[25]

Then, Galatians 3:28 illustrates God's intentions for the life of His Church: *"There is neither Jew nor Gentile, neither slave nor free, nor is there male and female, for you are all one in Christ Jesus."* And besides, the patriarchal role of senior pastor wasn't supposed to be normative (intended from creation); it is in fact a result of the fall.[26] And Jesus redeemed both women and men from the fall.

I also would have respectfully told my ministry leader that if God gave spiritual gifts to only men, the three scriptural passages that enumerate the gifts (1 Corinthians 12, Ephesians 4, and Romans 12) would have also been gender specific. Additionally, if the gifts appear in order of hierarchy, the Scriptures list apostle first, giving that gift of ministry greater weight. And Paul himself cited *Junia*, a woman, as

---

[25] Loren Cunningham and David Joel Hamilton, *Why Not Women?* (Seattle: Youth with a Mission Publishing, 2000), p. 93.

[26] Deborah M. Gill, *Biblical Theology of Women in Leadership.*

one of the early church apostles.[27] Along the same thought pattern, Paul mentions prophecy in all three lists of gifts. Women clearly prophesied in the Bible.

Moreover, an attack against women ministers constitutes an attack against the character of God. God created both male and female—in His image.[28] When the enemy devalues either gender, he attempts to devalue Almighty God. When the enemy dilutes the call of women ministers, he tries to dilute the blood of Jesus and the power of the cross.[29] Jesus died for all—men and women alike. God is the *shatterer* of glass ceilings!

As the conversation with the person to whom I looked for leadership concluded, I held back my tears, expressed my gratefulness for the time taken (good manners equals good ministry), and walked out of the meeting as quickly as I could. Safely in my car, though, hot tears flowed down my face and stung my cheeks. I had walked into the meeting

---

[27] "Greet Andronicus and Junia, my fellow Jews who have been in prison with me. They are outstanding among the apostles, and they were in Christ before I was" (Romans 16:7).

[28] Genesis 1:27.

[29] Loren Cunningham and David Joel Hamilton, *Why Not Women?* (Seattle: Youth with a Mission Publishing, 2000), p. 43.

exhilarated; but I walked out more devastated and disappointed than I had ever been in my entire life.

God lovingly wrapped His arms around me, though, and whispered, "Trust Me; trust Me, trust *Me*. The very person who you thought would obstruct your call will be the very person I will use to launch you into full-time ministry. When I promote you, people will say, 'Only God could have done that!' "

God places all kinds of people in our lives. Some become so powerful to us that they energize us as soon as they walk into a room, and other people deplete us. However if we are wise we will learn from them all.

The mentors God placed in my life during those days were women like Joyce Meyer, Naomi Dowdy, and Marilyn Hickey. Although far away from me in geographic distance, they served as mentors in living form instead of simply through pages of their books. I spent thousands of dollars to attend their conferences to purposely position myself for encouragement. While others took notes of their sermons, I noted how they carried themselves, conducted their ministries, dealt with problems that arose, and interacted with their staff.

On April 23, 2004, I had a dream that set many events into motion. In the dream I saw a block calendar like one used as a desk blotter. The day of April 26 lifted off the page, became three-dimensional, and huge. The dream ended as quickly as it started, but God was clearly preparing me for something big.

A few days later, as I read my email messages, I came across a newsletter from an evangelism ministry. It read: "Domain name Evangelize.com for sale—$1,000." I knew God wanted me to buy the domain, so I offered to purchase it for $500.

The owners responded that they had already received a full price offer of $1,000 from the Methodist Church (not *a* church, but the Methodist denomination) and that they were going to take their offer. I replied and told them to please contact me if they changed their minds, or if the other party reneged. I couldn't compete with the resources of an entire denomination, but I knew God could.

A couple of hours later, I received a follow-up message from them accepting my offer of $500. They said that God instructed them to sell it to me because I would use it to win souls. I shouted in jubilance as I read the message, and then I realized it was April 26, the date that "something big" was going to happen.

I proceeded to build a website—Evangelize. com. It was painstaking because I am not technologically gifted; but by the grace of God, I learned HTML codes in order to launch a website dedicated to training Christians how to win souls. It also had a companion email newsletter, *A Passion for Souls*, which provided monthly witnessing inspiration and practical tips. It went to people in fifty nations around the world.

Meanwhile, a friend who operates in the gift of prophecy approached me. She said that because I was going to be in full-time ministry, I should have personal intercessors to provide a prayer covering for me. I took her prophetic word seriously and asked God to supply the need. A few months later, my friend JoAnn Kates informed me that God had given her the mandate to pray for me until she took her last breath.

History demonstrates the importance of prayer coverings. Father Daniel Nash preceded Charles Finney, the leader of the Second Great Awakening, into every city where Finney preached. Nash then interceded for Finney and his crusade, so that when Finney arrived in town, the spiritual ground was already tilled. Church history credits Nash as one of the reasons for Finney's great success.[30] Charles Finney had Father Nash; I have JoAnn Kates.

I rejoice that God has provided a personal intercessor to cover me in prayer. JoAnn intercedes for me daily—whenever I have a preaching engagement, as I write every paper for my doctorate, and as the Lord gives her pause. Several others also form what I call my *prayer shield*, but JoAnn Kates remains my principle intercessor. I couldn't fulfill my calling without JoAnn answering hers.

One day as JoAnn interceded for me, she received a passage of Scripture for me. With consternation, JoAnn explained to me what she had received from God. It was Joshua 1:6-9.

God was preparing me for a new ministry—leadership. Joshua's marching orders were becoming

---

[30] J. Paul Reno, "Daniel Nash 1775-1831 Prayer Warrior for Charles Finney," accessed April 14, 2018. https://hopefaithprayer.com/prayer-warrior-charles-finney/.

mine, and the season in which my focus was exclusively on evangelism was coming to a close.

Questions for Reflection – Chapter 6

1. What helped you from this chapter? What gave you a different perspective? What surprised you the most?

_____

_____

_____

_____

_____

_____

_____

_____

2. What is your life's verse and why?

_____

_____

_____

_____

_____

_____

_____

3. Finish this sentence pertaining to your call: "If you cut me, I bleed _____."

4. If someone gave you $1 million, how would you spend it?

_____

_____

_____

_____

_____

_____

_____

5. Think about all the activities that incorporate your life. When do you feel most alive? What do you do for God that makes you feel the most energized?

_____

_____

_____

_____

_____

_____

_____

6. Think about all of the different aspects of ministry in which you have been involved. What ministry have you been the most passionate about?

_____

_____

_____

_____

_____

_____

_____

_____

_____

7. There will always be those who discount you for ministry. How will you respond when it happens to you?

_____

_____

_____

_____

_____

_____

_____

8. Wise protégés will learn from every mentor God places in their lives. What have been the most powerful lessons you have learned from your mentors?

_____

_____

_____

_____

_____

_____

_____

_____

_____

_____

_____

_____

_____

_____

_____

_____

_____

_____

9. Have you received any words of prophecy which have pointed to your call? If so, share them here.

_____

_____

_____

_____

_____

_____

_____

_____

_____

_____

_____

_____

_____

_____

_____

_____

_____

_____

10. God had asked me to trust Him and not look at my discouraging circumstances. In what areas is God asking you to trust Him with regard to your call?

_____

_____

_____

_____

_____

_____

_____

_____

_____

_____

_____

_____

_____

_____

_____

_____

_____

_____

_____

_____

11. Intercessory prayer is the immune system for your ministry. Who is on your prayer team?

_____

_____

_____

_____

_____

_____

_____

_____

_____

_____

_____

_____

_____

_____

_____

_____

_____

_____

_____

_____

_____

7

THE MINISTRY OF LEADERSHIP

My leadership verse:

Be strong and very courageous. Be careful to obey all the law my servant Moses gave you; do not turn from it to the right or to the left, that you may be successful wherever you go. Keep this book of the Law always on your lips; meditate on it day and night, so that you may be careful to do everything written in it. Then you will be prosperous and successful. Have I not commanded you? Be strong and courageous. Do not be afraid;

do not be discouraged, for the Lord your God will be with you wherever you go. —Joshua 1:6-9

In June 2006, I received a call from my sectional presbyter. The conversation we had during that call changed the course of my life. He explained that a church in our geographic section, Calvary Assembly of God (CAG) in Williamstown, New Jersey, had suddenly lost their pastor; and he asked if I would fill the pulpit as guest speaker the next Sunday. I agreed with elation and preached that Sunday at CAG.

Several months later, my presbyter called me again. This time he asked if I would consider serving as their interim pastor. Honored and excited, I agreed to lead as interim pastor of CAG, even though it was a dying church.

Sometimes the greatest opportunities are those no one else wants.

CAG was sixty years old, and every ministry had dwindled and ended, except their Sunday morning service. For twenty years the church had steadily declined. I began as interim pastor with twelve people in attendance. The church had been given a terminal diagnosis, and everyone to whom I turned for encouragement described the situation as bleak and hopeless.

I rolled up my sleeves, prayed hard, and worked tirelessly, co-laboring with God to turn CAG into a thriving congregation. It takes a certain kind of personality to revitalize a church. It requires spiritual toughness along with a let's-get-things-done attitude to pull a dying church out of a spiritual ditch.

At the end of the six-month interim period, the congregation of CAG requested me as their permanent senior pastor. Rules did not permit an interim pastor to become the senior pastor, but the district decided to make an exception for this particular situation. I was finally in full-time ministry.

When I was officially offered the senior pastor position, I said, "If you are looking for someone to lead a funeral procession until CAG gasps its last breath, I am not the pastor for whom you are looking. But if you are looking for a pastor who believes that God will breathe new life into CAG, and that our future days will be greater than anything in the past, I will do it!"

On April 22, 2007, I became the senior pastor of Calvary Assembly of God. What a day of rejoicing it was! After waiting for eighteen years, I had finally stepped into my calling to full-time ministry. When God opens a door for you, don't stagger through, don't walk through, don't hold onto the doorjamb, but *R-U-N* through the door of opportunity He has given you!

My husband, son, and I commuted from our home to the church forty-five minutes each way. We knew we would have to move closer and take a true risk selling the beautiful home we had built—the one we thought we would live in forever. To make matters worse, the real estate market had plummeted. The value of our house dropped by $20,000. We needed every penny of that $20,000 to afford the move. Nevertheless, by faith, we placed our Fairton, New Jersey, house on the market and began searching for a home in Williamstown, New Jersey. Then we waited for God to perform a miracle.

And He did.

One morning, a few months later, the phone rang. The person calling identified himself as a Hollywood producer and writer. He explained that in addition to his work in Hollywood, he was also a Christian who produced three-minute short films for ministry. He wanted to purchase my domain name, Evangelize.com, to market his films. Around the same time, I had been praying regarding the future of my website. God had mightily used it for five years to win souls, but pastoring was time intensive, and the information on the website grew stale.

A few days after his initial call, the Hollywood producer wired $20,000 into my checking account to purchase the domain. That, coupled with an offer we received from a buyer for our home, was the miracle for which my husband and I had waited. We purchased a home a mere eight minutes from the church, allowing us to live in the community where we pastored.

I have learned this about God: He is a multi-tasker! He will bring to pass many, many, many things from one.

After moving, I continued to work hard. I trained volunteers and established the church's mission, vision, and core values. I developed a discipleship strategy that included small groups and a two-year leadership school that serves as the leadership training pipeline of our church. The church began growing, which yielded the fruit of our labor. God has turned our church around and restored it to health.

In January 2014, God led us to change the name of our church. During a personal retreat, God led me to Ezekiel 37:1-14. Ezekiel speaks life to dry bones in that passage of Scripture. Then God expounded the following to me:

> When everyone around you saw death at Calvary Assembly of God, you saw life. You told everyone who would listen that I was going to breathe new life into the church. The calling on Calvary Assembly of God is to see life in that which is dead. I have called this church to collect as many dead people as you can find. You are to speak life, pray life, preach life, and teach them how to walk the abundant life. I have done a new thing; I have changed your name. Formerly you were known as Dead Church; your new name is Life Church.

The Lord told me our church would collect the dead—those who were dead in their callings, in their hopes, and in their dreams—and our church's new name was to reflect what God had done in our church to bring them back to life.

In October of 2015, a nationally syndicated Christian radio show invited me to be their guest to discuss the topic, "Should Christians Celebrate Halloween?" I flew to the Midwest, and when I arrived at the station, the staff quickly ushered me into a room and apprised me of a turn of events. The vice president of the radio station learned that a female pastor was being interviewed and asked the host to cancel me.

The host of the radio show refused to cancel my appearance because the show wasn't addressing the issue of female pastors. The vice president conceded but with a stipulation: I couldn't be introduced with the title of "pastor."

As was prophesied ten years earlier, I came to need the strong leadership legs that God had given me in order to stand firm in His call on my life. That occasion serves as only one example of the many challenges I have faced as a female pastor, and I am not alone in these challenges.

For a class paper I wrote for my doctorate, I interviewed twenty Assemblies of God female senior pastors regarding their unique leadership challenges. Additionally, I interviewed seventeen Assemblies of God district superintendents. The superintendents have a bird's-eye view of the challenges that women pastors in their districts encounter.

The challenges voiced by the women I interviewed fell into six themes. They are:

- Cultural and historic biases
- Lack of camaraderie and fellowship with male colleagues
- Absence of mentoring
- Balancing ministry and family
- Insecurity
- Leadership challenges common to both genders

Insecurity proves to be the greatest challenge. And to conquer insecurity we must learn to die to *self.* Dying to self and knowing who we are in Christ is crucial to effective pastoring. The lives of two of the female pastors I interviewed illustrate that God gives us the ability to overcome that and every challenge.

Cheri Sampson is the senior pastor of Salt River Indian Assembly of God, which is located on a Native American Indian reservation in Scottsdale, Arizona. She is also the first Native American woman in Assemblies of God history to be elected to the position of sectional presbyter. Sampson affirms that "self" is her greatest leadership challenge.

Cheri told me of an extremely hurtful incident that happened to her over thirty years ago, when someone in authority discounted her ministry. More noteworthy than the painful incident itself, though, was the lesson the Lord taught her after it happened. Here is what she recounted:

Jesus came and sat right beside me. I felt deep inside myself His voice saying, "Cheri, the only person who can stop what I am going to do in your life is you." Suddenly I realized that "I" stopped "me." My insecurities stopped me. My attitudes stopped me. My thoughts of "you're a Native American, a woman, too fat, too ugly, not talented," stopped me. At that moment, I repented and asked the Lord to forgive me for not believing Him. It was as if a light switch went on in my head. I had a God confidence and knew that nothing or no one could stop what God would do in my life but "me!" If a person does not want to work with me because I am Native American, that is their challenge. If a person does not want to work with me because I am a woman, that is their challenge. It is not men, women, the Church, the District, or General Council that is the problem. The challenge is self— stinkin' self![31]

Pastor Sampson shared with me how she overcomes this challenge. She said, "Dying daily to my opinions, my attitudes, my thoughts, and my desires and allowing God to give me everything I need to be a true reflection of Him is how I counteract this.

---

[31] Cheri Sampson, Senior Pastor of Salt River Indian Assembly of God, Scottsdale, AZ, interview by author, email message, January 22, 2016.

God's approval is now what I long for and I stay in His presence until I have that assurance."

Then there was Pastor Ellen Blackwell, whom I had the privilege of including in the interviews when she was 102 years old. Pastor Blackwell passed away in January 2018 at the age of 104—the longest living female minister in the Assemblies of God. She held the position of senior pastor for over seventy years. Even after seven decades of pastoring, she couldn't name one challenge as a female senior pastor. When I asked why, this is what said:

From the time I received the penetrating and glorious baptism in the Holy Spirit I had to tell everyone within the radius of my life about Jesus. I was never satisfied to sit down with the Gospel. I took off in one direction or another. I traveled all over the eastern United States telling people about Him. I didn't have time or occasion to think of gender or problems. I cared for my flock and lost myself in the indwelling Christ while continually discovering new open doors. I was always busy opening new areas. When you are a pioneer, no one gets in your way, and you don't get in anyone else's way either![32]

One of the district superintendents I interviewed didn't point to church culture or church boards as the cause of discouragement and challenge for women ministers, but to women themselves. He believes the single greatest obstacle to women serving as pastors is that women are waiting for someone else to open the door for them to serve. A man has already opened the door for anyone called to the ministry— His name is Jesus!

If God has called us, He will open doors and provide ways for us to pursue our callings. When Jesus died on the cross, He not only provided the way for us to be saved, but He also opened the door for all of us to be guided by the Holy Spirit. My ministry journey is comprised of God opening one door of opportunity after the next as I've learned to follow and respond to the Holy Spirit's guidance.

---

[32] Ellen Blackwell, Senior Pastor of Mount Zion Assembly of God, Charles Town, WV, interview by author, email message, January 25, 2016,

One fallacy with which female pastors contend is based on the idea of a *zero-sum game*. If a game is known to be a zero-sum game, there is never a gain by one player that is not balanced by the other player's loss. Winning is always balanced by losing. Applied by some people, this theory states that "power can never increase or decrease but always remains constant."[33] Applied in a flawed, theological manner, this theory suggests that when a woman occupies a biblical leadership position, one less position exists for men. The Great Commission, however, remains in full force for all of us—and when everyone's power grows, so the Church grows.[34]

Another ridiculous theological argument used to weaken the ministries of women senior pastors is that when a man is not willing, available, or suitable, it forces God to choose a woman.[35] Sunday school classes and pulpits around the world have taught this, and it has been used to minimize the calling and ministry of the Old Testament's Deborah (one

---

[33] Deborah M. Gill and Barbara Cavaness, *God's Women Then and Now* (Colorado Springs: Authentic Books, 2009), p. 181.
[34] Ibid.
[35] Marg Mowczko, *Deborah and the No Available Men Argument*, accessed April 14, 2018, http://newlife.id.au/equality-and-gender-issues/deborah-and-the-no-available-men-argument/.

of the judges of Israel) and refute the thought that God calls women into leadership roles over men.

God handpicked Deborah, a prophet, judge, and leader of Israel, to preserve the nation.[36] The absurd argument that women remain God's second choice scathingly insults God's character and power. While the Bible contains accounts of men who seemed unavailable, unwilling, or felt unsuitable for God's divine assignment, God does not relegate the calls He places upon women as His "Plan B" in dealing with them. God's power can break through every obstacle to one's calling—just as He did with Jonah the prophet.[37]

God chooses whom He chooses for the work of ministry. The prophet represents God to the people; therefore, the people do not get to choose the prophet. Biblical and contemporary history has shown that if the people do not like the prophet or the prophet's message, they want to stone the prophet (literally or figuratively).[38] Nevertheless God does the choosing.

God chose Deborah, and He has chosen me!

---

[36] Chapters 4 and 5 of Judges.

[37] Read the book of Jonah to see how God has His way even with reluctant and disobedient men.

[38] Deborah M. Gill, "Biblical Theology of Women in Leadership."

My mentors during my journey into maturing as a leader consisted of Drs. Wayne and Sherry Lee of Church Life Cohorts, Dr. Mark Rutland, and the professors of Oral Roberts University (ORU). For two years I met with Wayne and Sherry Lee on a monthly basis for pastoral coaching. I attended Dr. Rutland's National Institute of Christian Leadership for one year, and upon completion of my coursework I obtained a master of arts degree in practical theology from ORU.

My admission to Oral Roberts University was a significant miracle that God wrought in my life. When the Lord instructed me to pursue a master's degree it seemed impossible—and for good reason. You see, I never obtained a bachelor's degree, only my associate's degree. It is unheard of to be accepted into an accredited master's degree program without having earned a bachelor's degree. But God assured me that if I applied, I would be accepted into ORU's master's program, and He was right. God blasted open that door of opportunity!

By a miracle of God I received my acceptance letter! I completed the three-year program at ORU and graduated at the top of my class with a 4.0 GPA.

The Lord was true to the words He whispered in my ear that day in the midst of my discouragement— yes, only God!

To Him be the glory for the great things He has done!

Then, in time, the Lord began moving me into another season of learning as yet another phase of my ministry journey was soon to begin. God once again inspired my personal intercessor JoAnn Kates to give to me more words from Him for my direction. Those words are contained in verses 4 through 10 of Jeremiah chapter 1. That passage, which God shared with JoAnn while she was interceding for me, captures a snapshot of the sacred *call encounter* that Jeremiah had with God.

God called Jeremiah to be a prophet to the nations and bring a needed reformation to the people of God. The weighty mantle that God placed upon Jeremiah included preaching an unpopular message to people who had hardened spiritual hearts and deaf spiritual ears.

As JoAnn read that passage of Scripture to me, I knew a more challenging season was about to begin; it proved both awe inspiring and daunting at the same time. Whenever we go to a new level in God, our eyes must adjust to see what God is doing.

Questions for Reflection – Chapter 7

1. What helped you from this chapter? What gave you a different perspective? What surprised you the most?

_____

_____

_____

_____

_____

_____

_____

_____

_____

_____

_____

_____

_____

_____

_____

_____

_____

_____

2. Waiting for God's perfect time to begin your ministry can be extremely difficult. We often feel prepared to answer His call long before God knows we are ready. The temptation to push a door open is great—however, we must always wait for God to open the door. Describe a time when you pushed a door open before God's appointed time (or a time you were tempted to).

_____

_____

_____

_____

_____

_____

_____

_____

_____

_____

_____

_____

_____

_____

_____

_____

_____

3. Preparation is never lost time—it is extremely valuable. Why does it feel like you are wasting time when you are in a season of preparation?

_____

_____

_____

_____

_____

_____

_____

_____

4. Describe what might happen if someone endeavors to skip over God's preparation season for their lives and launch themselves into ministry before they are ready.

_____

_____

_____

_____

_____

_____

_____

_____

5. There is a difference between being called into ministry and being released into ministry. Explain.

_____

_____

_____

_____

_____

_____

_____

_____

_____

_____

6. What are your spiritual gifts?

_____

_____

_____

_____

_____

_____

_____

_____

_____

_____

7. What are your greatest talents and natural abilities?

_____

_____

_____

_____

_____

_____

_____

_____

_____

_____

8. What results have you received from personality or giftings tests that helped to point to your call?

_____

_____

_____

_____

_____

_____

_____

_____

_____

_____

9. What are symptoms of insecurity?

_____

_____

_____

_____

_____

_____

_____

_____

_____

_____

10. How can insecurity hinder your call?

_____

_____

_____

_____

_____

_____

_____

_____

_____

11. How is insecurity counteracted?

_____

_____

_____

_____

_____

_____

_____

_____

_____

_____

_____

_____

8

The Ministry of Prayer

My prayer verse:

> The word of the Lord came to me, saying,
> "Before I formed you in the womb I knew you,
> before you were born I set you apart; I appointed
> you as a prophet to the nations."
>
> "Ah, Sovereign Lord," I said, "I do not know
> how to speak; I am only a child."
>
> But the Lord said to me, "Do not say, 'I am
> only a child.' You must go to everyone I send you
> to and say whatever I command you. Do not be

afraid of them, for I am with you and will rescue you," declares the Lord.

Then the Lord reached out his hand and touched my mouth and said to me, "Now, I have put my words in your mouth. See, today I appoint you over nations and kingdoms to uproot and tear down, to destroy and overthrow, to build and to plant." —Jeremiah 1:4-10

In March 2014, I visited Israel for the first time. While walking through Jerusalem with my tour group, I heard the Muslim call to prayer in person for the first time. Prior to that, I had heard it only on television or in the movies. To say that it felt eerie to me gravely understates the experience. The Muslim call to prayer expressed the shrillest, emptiest, and most hollow sound that I have ever heard in my life.

I not only heard it, I felt it. My spirit felt sick. I looked around the group to see if anyone else had the same reaction; they did not. I realized that the rest of my tour group also heard the Muslim call to prayer but only with their physical ears. They paid the same attention to it as one would to a fire engine's siren; they heard it and quickly dismissed it.

I then realized that God allowed me to hear it with my spiritual ears.

And He got my attention.

I asked, "Lord, why am I having this reaction?"

He responded, "What the Muslims describe a *call to prayer*, I call *a call to death*."

He continued, "I am raising up leaders and houses of prayer all around the world to call the Church back to the place of prayer."

I felt stunned, honored, and overwhelmed all at the same time.

The tour continued to the Garden of Gethsemane. As tourists do, we had our cameras poised to snap pictures of the place where Jesus prayed as He faced His crucifixion. In the middle of this photo opportunity, God began speaking to me again.

"When Jesus needed the prayers of His disciples the most, they fell asleep," He said to me. "When I need My Church praying the most, My Church is asleep to prayer."

Then God spoke something similar to what He had told me earlier in Old City, Jerusalem. "I am raising up leaders all around the world to call the Church back to the place of prayer, and you are one of them. I am raising up houses of prayer all around the world to pray for revival in these last days, and Life Church in Williamstown, New Jersey, is one of them."

Shortly after returning home from the trip, and while doing course work for my studies at ORU, I had another encounter with God regarding what I now call my *prayer calling*. As I was writing a paper on Church history, the Lord made it abundantly clear that the reason He had called me to obtain my graduate degree was to study the life of reformers and revivalists. I was acutely aware that God would use me, along with many others, to bring a prayer-reformation to the Church. The prayer awakening would serve as a precursor to worldwide revival.

God impressed upon me the first place to start. I was to launch a regional house of prayer as a ministry of my church, Life Church. This regional, 24/7 house of prayer would offer space for intercessors in our region to cry out to the Lord for a prayer awakening, revival, and souls.

One and a half years after my trip to Israel, on October 17, 2015, we dedicated the Life House of Prayer (LHOP) to the Lord. LHOP includes one room for corporate prayer and two personal prayer rooms, each equipped with comfortable seating. iPads loaded with worship music are in each room in addition to anointing oil, communion elements, prayer guides, and objects to help intercessors engage in prayer. Intercessors who serve in LHOP reserve prayer slots in one-hour increments on our website at http://lifeishere.org/lhop/.

In addition to launching our 24/7 house of prayer, I wrote the book, *The Life House of Prayer and the History of 24/7 Prayer.* I have also written articles on the topic of prayer for both *Charisma* magazine and *The Christian Post.* And my story about the Life House of Prayer was featured in the online version of *Pentecostal Evangel News*—now *AG News*, https://news.ag.org/.

I also have the honor of being a member of America's National Prayer Committee (NPC). The NPC is an invitation-only group of the largest and most influential prayer ministries in America. The National Prayer Committee provides leadership to the National Day of Prayer.

Then in March 2017 I received a call from Mark Forrester of the Assemblies of God Headquarters in Springfield, Missouri. Mark explained that the Executive Leadership Team had approved a five-member Assembly of God Prayer Committee to help raise a culture of prayer in local churches, district offices, and national headquarters. Mark continued by asking me to be a part of that committee. I literally held the receiver away from my head and screamed loudly. When I returned the phone to my ear, Mark was laughing on the other end. I just couldn't contain my elation; once again God had done what He promised to do.

As I entered into and continued to mature in my calling to the ministry of prayer my mentors in developing prayer ministries included Anne Graham Lotz, Dick Eastman, Dutch Sheets, and others who have received their own prayer mandates from God. Cheryl Salem and Cindy Jacobs have also been mentors to me. I study their prayer strategies, read their books, and follow their social media posts for daily encouragement. From afar, they encourage, inspire and challenge me to *soldier on* in this calling.

Questions for Reflection – Chapter 8

1. What helped you from this chapter? What gave you a different perspective? What surprised you the most?

_____

_____

_____

_____

_____

_____

_____

_____

2. Describe any God-encounters, dreams, or visions you have had regarding your purpose in life.

_____

_____

_____

_____

_____

_____

_____

_____

3. What peoples group(s) are you called to reach?

_____

_____

_____

_____

_____

_____

_____

_____

4. Christians are Kingdom builders. What part of building God's Kingdom do you see yourself playing?

_____

_____

_____

_____

_____

_____

_____

_____

5. God has a blueprint in heaven with every detail of your calling recorded. What steps do you take to find out what it shows?

_____

_____

_____

_____

_____

_____

_____

_____

6. What details of the blueprint has God already revealed to you?

_____

_____

_____

_____

_____

_____

_____

_____

7. When we meet Jesus face-to-face, we long to hear from our Savior these words, "Well done, good and faithful servant." This implies that we did what God asked us to do, we did it well, and we exhibited faithfulness while doing it. How can we let eternity compel us to fulfill our life's mission?

_____

_____

_____

_____

_____

_____

8. Read and meditate on Isaiah 30:21 and Proverbs 3:5-6. Share what you feel God is showing you with regard to the actions He would have you take regarding your calling.

_____

_____

_____

_____

_____

_____

9. On a scale of 1 to 10, how ready are you to take action steps regarding God's call? _____

10. Until now, what has kept you from moving forward in God's call?

_____

_____

_____

_____

_____

_____

_____

_____

_____

_____

_____

_____

_____

_____

PART 3

MY FUTURE MINISTRY

9

THE CONVERGENCE OF MINISTRIES

The previous times of learning and discovery spent in my ministry journey have prepared me for the season in which I presently stand. God blends the threads of my past and intertwines the strands of my future to create a beautiful ministry tapestry. And He has graciously given me a glimpse of that weave.

After years of full-time ministry I have come to the conclusion that one of the secrets to greatness is to be brilliantly simple. If we stay in the lane to which God has called us, we will live a life of growth, fruitfulness, and productivity. Weaving, bobbing, and changing ministry lanes cause double-minded-ness, barrenness, and confusion.

The three stages of learning and expansion in my ministry journey—evangelism, leadership, and prayer—have also been the three *themes* of my life. The one-lane highway upon which God has posi-tioned me on my journey leads in only one direction. And my successful progression on it towards the goal centers on this proclamation of my faith:

I am called to fan the flame of revival and mentor trailblazer leaders to set the world on fire for Jesus Christ!

God had to immerse me in three specific stages of spiritual growth in order to gloriously blend them together for use in both my present ministry and that of the future. Just as three-part harmony cannot exist without three accomplished vocalists, my future as evangelist, pastor, and prayer leader could not be what it is without these three phases of ministry.

If I could describe my calling now in the context of historical Christian leaders it would be something like, Jeremiah the prophet meets pastor/evangelist William Seymour, who, together, encounter the 24/7 praying Moravians![39]

In May 2015, when I graduated from ORU with my master's degree, I participated in the school of theology's hooding ceremony. As my professors placed the hood around my neck, I sensed God placing a new apostolic and prophetic mantle on my life. I believe God has anointed me, and my church, to take cities, regions, and nations for Him.

In addition, God has called me to write for Him. I already mentioned writing articles for *Charisma News*, *The Christian Post*, *Discipleship Journal*, *The Upper Room*, *Fox News*, and the *Pentecostal Evangel*. But in addition to that, my article, "50 Reasons Why I Don't Drink," was shared on social media over 1.5 million times and was *Charisma News'* most popular article in 2016 and 2017. One of the reasons God breathed on that article was to confirm my calling as a writer. God assured me that if I obediently

---

[39] "The Moravian Community of Herrnhut in Saxony, in 1727, commenced a round-the-clock 'prayer watch' that continued nonstop for over a hundred years."
https://christianhistoryinstitute.org/magazine/article/one-hundred-year-prayer-meeting, accessed April 14, 2018.

answered the calling of author, He would cause whatever I wrote to get into the hands of those who need it.

I am called to pastor the wonderful people at Life Church. I will teach them to pray, win souls, and position them for revival. I will ready them for the last days, prepare them for dealing with persecution that is sure to come, and encourage them to stand firm until the end. God has called me to pastor the remnant, and, together, we will be a voice in the wilderness calling, *"Prepare the way for the Lord!"*[40]

In conjunction with my calling as pastor, I will continue to lead the Life House of Prayer. Prayer permeates everything we do. We offer multiple opportunities for prayer, conduct rhythms of 24/7 prayer, and fast and pray for worldwide revival and the salvation of souls and nations. The Life House of Prayer is the prayer expression of Life Church.

And like Paul the apostle, God calls me to evangelize the nations with all boldness and without hindrance.[41] Like Jeremiah the prophet and

---

[40] Mark 1:3.

[41] "Boldly and without hindrance he preached the kingdom of God and taught about the Lord Jesus Christ" (Acts 28:31).

reformer, I am God's reformer sent to demolish the sin of prayerlessness in the Church.[42] Like Joshua the leader, I will lead and strategize both evangelism and prayer, and lead many people to the Promised Land.[43]

And God is going to fan the flame of revival around the world!

---

[42] Jeremiah 1:7-10.

[43] "After the death of Moses the servant of the Lord, the Lord said to Joshua son of Nun, Moses' aide: "Moses my servant is dead. Now then, you and all these people, get ready to cross the Jordan River into the land I am about to give to them—to the Israelites. I will give you every place where you set your foot, as I promised Moses. Your territory will extend from the desert to Lebanon, and from the great river, the Euphrates—all the Hittite country—to the Great Sea on the west. No one will be able to stand up against you all the days of your life. As I was with Moses, so I will be with you; I will never leave you nor forsake you.

"Be strong and courageous, because you will lead these people to inherit the land I swore to their forefathers to give them" (Joshua 1:1-6).

Questions for Reflection – Chapter 9

1. What helped you from this chapter? What gave you a different perspective? What surprised you the most?

_____

_____

_____

_____

_____

_____

_____

_____

_____

_____

_____

_____

2. To realize the greatest possible growth, fruitfulness, and productivity we must stay in our ministry lane. A way to do this is to craft a one-sentence mission statement. Our mission statement will act as a plumb line with which we measure opportunities

and decisions. To help craft your mission statement, ask yourself these four questions:

- What am I called to do?
- Who are the people that I am called to reach?
- What does God want to do through me?
- What desired outcome or end result does God want to see?

As an example, here is how I answered these four questions for my mentoring ministry:

- I am a mentor. (What am I called to do?)
- I help eternally minded trailblazer leaders. (Who are the people I am called to reach?)
- To identify their unique calling. (What does God want to do through me?)
- So more laborers will be thrust into the harvest field. (What is the desired result?)

Here is my mentoring mission statement:

I am a mentor. I help eternally minded, trail-blazer leaders to identify their unique calling so that more laborers will be thrust into the harvest field.

3. Now let's craft your mission statement. Answer these four questions:

- I am a _____

  _____.

  (What am I called to do?)

- I help_____

  _____.

  (Who are the people I am called to reach?)

- To _____

  _____.

  (What does God want to do through you?)

- So _____

_____.

(What is the desired result?)

4. Using my mentoring mission statement as a guide, put the above four sentences together, and write your mission statement here:

_____

_____

_____

_____

_____

_____

_____

_____

_____

_____

_____

_____

_____

_____

_____

_____

_____

In order to fulfill your mission, action steps must be taken. Create a minimum of three action steps accompanied by personal deadlines for accomplishment:

<u>**Action Step**</u>   <u>**Deadline**</u>

1. _____   _____

2. _____   _____

3. _____   _____

4. _____   _____

5. _____   _____

6. _____   _____

7. _____   _____

8. _____   _____

9. _____   _____

10. _____   _____

10

A WORLDWIDE PLATFORM

One day I was complaining to God about the huge platform minister *so-and-so* has. I lamented, "If I had a platform as big as hers, I could reach more people for You."

I never expected God to answer my tale of woe, but He did.

"Who gave her that platform?" He cut right to the chase.

"Well . . . You did, Lord," I humbly replied.

God has a way of encouraging and correcting us all at the same time.

"Can I give *YOU* a platform?" He poignantly asked.

"Yes, Lord, of course. You can do anything."

At that point I knew that what seemed like a mountain was beginning to turn into a miracle. Hope was welling up inside of me.

Then God ended His part of our discourse with two, powerful words: "Ask Me."

I paused for a moment to catch my breath. If God told me to ask, I was going to ask big. Small requests are an insult to our mighty God.

"God, I ask You for a platform as wide as the world!"

As far as I am concerned, it is now a done deal—end of conversation.

Since that day, God has given me glimpses of the platform He has in store for me. He is also teaching me how precious a God-given platform is and how to steward it well.

Here are ten principles to help you steward well your own God-given platform:

1. A platform is what you stand on, where you stand, and the stand you have taken.

   • A platform is comprised of the vision, mission, and ministry God has given you. It is the vehicle from which the message God has given you gets out.

2. Don't try and build the platform yourself.

   • God is the giver of platforms. Like the *house* spoken of in Psalm 127, unless God builds the *platform* the laborers labor in vain.[44] Let Him build it in His perfect timing. Looking to man for that which only God can provide is a form of idolatry. We can manufacture a temporary platform with the arm of the flesh, but it will produce fleshly results. Only God can give you a platform that will result in eternal, lasting fruit.

---

[44] "Unless the Lord builds the house, its builders labor in vain" (Psalm 127:1).

3. Be faithful with the platforms that are right in front of you.

   - Look around. God has already given you platforms in your family, church, neighborhood, workplace, social media, and so forth. If you are faithful with the little platforms, God will give you bigger ones. Don't wait until you have a worldwide platform to do what God has called you to do; start right now where you are.

4. Make sure your motives are pure when asking God for a platform.

   - We have all seen examples of people (singers, actors, athletes, even some pastors) who ask God for a platform, but when they get it they use it for worldly purposes. When God gives you a platform, take care to use it for His glory. A great example of someone who has been faithful with her platform is my friend, Cheryl Prewitt Salem, Miss America 1980. Cheryl lifted high the name of Jesus during her entire one-year reign as Miss America. Today, thirty-six years later, as a former Miss America she is still using her platform to glorify God, and as a result, many souls have been won to the Kingdom. Unfortunately, this kind of platform stewardship can be rare. But know this: we will all be held accountable for the platforms God has given us.

5. Beware of standing on someone else's platform.

- If you are invited by a person, ministry, organization, movement, or political party to stand on an already-established platform other than the one you occupy, investigate that platform's building materials and the ground upon which it stands. Make certain the platform isn't constructed with compromising principles. Make sure it is built on sure, biblical precepts.

Don't stand on a flimsy platform built on shifting sand. Rock is solid; sand isn't.

6. Godly character is needed to sustain a godly platform.

   • Many Christians have fallen off of their platforms because they lacked the character of Christ. Men and women mightily anointed by God have trampled on their God-given platform due to compromised living. Allow God to mold and shape you into the image of His Son before He gives you a platform. Preparation is never lost time, but sorely needed for platform integrity and longevity.

7. Platforms look glamorous, but are anything but.

   • Nothing in the entire world compares to standing on your God-given platform. There is joy unspeakable when you are living God's dream for your

life! But there is also hurt, persecution, disappointments, and fiery trials
there. At times you will feel drained
and diminished, and you will feel like
quitting. Learn the much-needed skill
of encouraging yourself in the Lord.
If you don't, disillusionment can set in
and sabotage your platform. Standing
on the right platform may not be glamorous, but Jesus is worth anything we
must endure on our platform!

8. God will use people to help construct
your platform.

• You will stand on the shoulders of
those who have gone before you, and
God will give you a pastor, teachers,
and mentors to speak into your life.
He will use some of them to construct
things that need building in your life.
He will use others to deconstruct that
which is not of Him. God will also give
you much-needed favor, resources, and

grace. Like Noah, trust and obey God throughout the building process.

9. The enemy will try to destroy your platform.

  • God uses people, but so does the devil. The enemy will send wolves in sheep's clothing, false prophets, offended people, hurting people—anyone who allows himself or herself to be used for evil purposes. It takes prayer and spiritual warfare to protect a platform. Ask God to assign anointed intercessors and watchmen to pray for you and your platform. Intercessors are like the immune system of the body of Christ; they protect it from foreign invaders and keep it healthy and strong. Through prayer, a watchman can stop the attack of the enemy before it even arrives.

10. Platforms are yours for the asking.

- Just as God used John the Baptist to prepare the way for the earthly ministry of Jesus,[45] God is calling each of us today to be a voice in the wilderness to prepare the way for the Second Coming of the Lord; and He yearns to give you a platform on which to proclaim the Gospel of Jesus Christ! I am convinced that in these last days, believers will not lack platforms; but instead, they will often lack the courage to climb their narrow stairs, the perseverance to continue standing in difficult times, and the purity of heart to take the necessary stand for righteousness!

I have found this season's mentors at the Assemblies of God Theological Seminary, where

---

[45] "Finally they said, 'Who are you? Give us an answer to take back to those who sent us. What do you say about yourself?'"

"John replied in the words of Isaiah the prophet, 'I am the voice of one calling in the desert, "Make straight the way for the Lord" ' " (John 1:22-23).

God has purposed for me to obtain a doctor of ministry. Dr. Deborah Gill, Dr. Carolyn Tennant, Dr. Lois Olena, Dr. Ava Oleson, and Dr. Cheryl Taylor pour into my life. God will use my professors, cohorts, books, papers, and assignments to mold and shape me. These are tools in the hands of the Potter to prepare me for my future season of ministry. Crystal Martin, National Director of Network of Women Ministers for the Assemblies of God, has imparted both life and wisdom to me. And Cindy Panepinto prophetically mentors me to uncover every aspect of the upward call God has placed on my life.

This book, like my journey to ministry, has caused both joy and pain as I have reflected on the events herein. Though at times taxing to relive, it has given me pause to reexamine the individual events that have comprised my life as a minister. God has used it mightily to connect the dots of my past and point to my future. The goodness of God remains the common thread throughout my journey.

I will be a minister of the Gospel until I take my last breath. Public opinion, fluctuations in denominational position, or changes in cultural climate will not halt me. I am an ordained minister of the Gospel and senior pastor of the Assemblies of God.

Questions for Reflection – Chapter 10

1. What helped you from this chapter? What gave you a different perspective? What surprised you the most?

_____

_____

_____

_____

_____

_____

_____

_____

_____

_____

_____

_____

2. Pride is lethal to your calling. If not eradicated, pride will cause you to fall off your God-given platform. Pride also blinds; you can possess pride in your heart and not recognize it. It is crucial that we ask God to expose any areas of pride in our heart and

routinely check our heart for pride. Here are some symptoms of pride. Be completely honest and put a check mark next to symptoms of pride that you exhibit:

- Are you always speaking of yourself?
- Do you try to impress? (There is nothing more impressive than humility.)
- Are you unhappy unless you are seen or noticed?
- How do you handle being ignored?
- Do you show genuine interest in other people?
- Are you a good listener?
- Do you interrupt frequently?
- Can you admit when you don't know something?
- Can you ask for help?
- Can you be honestly happy for someone who receives a material or spiritual blessing?
- Do you need a title or initials after your name to feel important?
- Do you cause strife? (Pride is an arguer; "I'm right and you're wrong.")

- Are you unnecessarily secretive about things?
- Do you get offended or get your feelings hurt easily?
- Can you be corrected by those in authority over you?
- Are you habitually late? (Pride doesn't care what time an event starts, only what time *you* want to arrive.)
- Are you more concerned with your plan for your life than God's?
- How well do you follow directions?
- Does it bother you to be second fiddle or subservient to someone?
- How do you handle someone else getting the credit for something you did?
- Can you handle it when someone else gets the promotion or position?
- Do you frequently get embarrassed?
- How well do you receive gifts? (Are you always the one that has to be giving but have a hard time receiving?)
- Do you have a difficult time publicly expressing your praise to God?

- Do you battle insecurity or low self-esteem?
  (Pride occurs when your eyes are on yourself,
  whether you think yourself higher, or lower,
  than you ought.)

3. God must always get the glory for any measure
of ministry success. How can you ensure that your
motives stay pure and that you don't keep the glory
for yourself? What can you do to intentionally give
glory to God when you receive accolades?

_____

_____

_____

_____

_____

_____

_____

_____

_____

_____

_____

_____

_____

_____

_____

4. Describe what can happen to a Christian leader who relies on their abilities, gifts, and talents, rather than 100 percent on the Lord?

_____

_____

_____

_____

_____

_____

_____

_____

_____

5. Unpack this thought: "I am a co-laborer with Christ, not a co-star."

_____

_____

_____

_____

_____

_____

_____

_____

_____

6. As we fulfill our call, our goal must be that people remember the name of Jesus, and forget our name. Practically speaking, how is this accomplished?

_____

_____

_____

_____

_____

_____

_____

_____

_____

7. What is the difference between doing things with excellence and perfectionism?

_____

_____

_____

_____

_____

_____

_____

_____

_____

8. Everyone needs a mentor and to be a mentor. Into whose life are you pouring into?

_____

_____

_____

_____

_____

_____

_____

9. Read and meditate on Acts 20:24. In your own words, write a prayer to God asking Him to make Acts 20:24 a reality in your life.

_____

_____

_____

_____

_____

_____

_____

_____

_____

_____

_____

10. Fast-forward five years from now. What does your life with regard to your calling look like? Be as detailed as possible as you see yourself, with your eyes of faith, fulfilling God's call on your life.

_____

_____

_____

_____

_____

_____

_____

_____

_____

_____

_____

_____

_____

_____

_____

_____

_____

_____

_____

_____

EPILOGUE

EMBRACING THE CALLING
OF PIONEER

Another aspect of my calling encompasses that of *pioneer*. Like Pastor Ellen Blackwell, who so boldly proclaimed her pioneering role, God has placed a similar mantle on my life. God calls me to defend women in ministry, both past and present, and stand as a gatekeeper and cheerleader for women in the present and future. As Ellen Blackwell was to me, I am to be to other women.

I am grateful to be a woman pastor in the Assemblies of God, a fellowship that has an egalitarian view of women in leadership. The Assemblies of God's official position asserts that God pours His Spirit upon both men and women equally.[46] In comparison to many other fellowships, the Assemblies of God affords women both rare and precious opportunities to lead.

The historical Azusa Street Revival[47] gave birth to the Assemblies of God; and in doing so it demolished all racial, socioeconomic, and gender norms.[48] As a result, the revival permitted 100 percent of the harvesters to go into the field to bring in the harvest.

Dr. Deborah Gill states, "There are fewer and fewer female models for younger women. Many of the women who feel called to ministry, and who begin to prepare for it, are discouraged by pastors,

---

[46] General Council of the Assemblies of God, *The Role of Women in Ministry as Described in Holy Scripture: A Position Paper of the General Council of the Assemblies of God*, General Council of the Assemblies of God, accessed April 14, 2018, https://ag.org/Beliefs/Topics-Index/The-Role-of-Women-in-Ministry/.

[47] The Azusa Street Revival took place in Los Angeles, California, beginning in 1906. It was led by William J. Seymour. The revival gave birth to what we know as twentieth-century Pentecostalism. People came from all over the world to experience the revival, whose nearly daily meetings lasted from 1906 to 1915. Because of this revival there are 800 million Pentecostal Christians on the earth today.

[48] Larry E. Martin, *The Life and Ministry of William J. Seymour* (Pensacola, FL: Christian Life Books, 2006), pp. 165-182.

educators, and denominational officials from pursuing their calling."[49]

I echo Dr. Gill's feelings and embrace the call of pioneer to women in ministry.

---

[49] Deborah M. Gill, "The Contemporary State of Women in Ministry in the Assemblies of God," p. 36.

RECOMMENDED READING

Arnold, Shirley, *Something Out of Nothing*.

Cavaness, Barbara and Deborah Gill, *God's Women Then and Now*.

Chand, Sam, *Leadership Pain*.

Cunningham, Loren and David Joel Hamilton, *Why Not Women: A Biblical Study of Women in Ministry, Missions, and Leadership*.

De Alminana, Margaret and Lois E. Olena, *Women in Pentecostal and Charismatic Ministry*.

Dowdy, Naomi, *Destiny Calling*.

Fleurant, Margie, *Focus: Eliminating Distractions for Enhanced Spiritual Vision*.

Fulthorp, Deborah. "Spirit-Empowered Women in Church Leadership: An Undergraduate Course for Southwestern Assemblies of God

University in Waxahachie, TX, with Local Church Implementation," Kindle edition.

Grady, J. Lee, *Ten Lies the Church Tells Women.*

Grenz, Stanley and Denis Muir Kjesbo, *Women in the Church.*

Hamon, Jane and Cindy Jacobs, *The Deborah Company.*

Lemley, Kristi, *Broken and Transformed: Moving Beyond Life's Difficult Times.*

Morgan, Jamie, *The Life House of Prayer and the History of 24/7 Prayer.*

Qualls, Joy E.A., *God Forgive Us for Being Women: Rhetoric, Theology, and the Role of Women in Pentecostal Tradition.*

Salem, Harry and Cheryl, *Distractions from Destiny: 8 Distractions You Must Overcome to Achieve Your Life's Purpose.*

Sparks, Donna, *Beauty from Ashes: My Story of Grace.*

About the Author

Jamie Morgan is an ordained minister of the Assemblies of God and lead pastor of Life Church in Williamstown, New Jersey. She obtained her master of arts degree in practical theology from Oral Roberts University and is currently pursuing a doctor of ministry degree from the Assemblies of God Theological Seminary. She is also a graduate of Dr. Mark Rutland's National Institute of Christian Leadership, a member of America's National Prayer Committee, and serves on the five-person Assemblies of God Prayer Committee.

Jamie is called to fan the flame of revival and mentor trailblazers to set the world on fire for Jesus Christ!

Pastor Jamie Morgan is the author of *The Life House of Prayer and the History of 24/7 Prayer* and has also been published in *Charisma News*, *The Christian Post*, the *Pentecostal Evangel*, *Fox News*, *Discipleship Journal*, *The Upper Room*, and other publications around the world. She is host of the television show, *Heal my Hurt*. Jamie is a wife, mother, mother-in-law, and grandmother. You can find out more about her at **JamieMorgan.com**.

Made in the USA
Columbia, SC
20 May 2018